Super Quick Origami Animals

Super Quick Origami Animals

Nick Robinson

Sterling Publishing Co., Inc.
New York

Creative director: Sarah King
Editor: Clare Haworth-Maden
Project editor: Sarah Harris
Designer: 2H Design

Library of Congress Cataloging-in-Publication Data Available

10   9   8   7   6   5   4   3   2   1

Published in 2002 by Sterling Publishing Company, Inc.
387 Park Avenue South, New York, N.Y. 10016

This book was designed and produced by
D&S Books
Cottage Meadow, Bocombe, Parkham
Bideford, Devon, EX39 5PH

© 2002 D&S Books

Distributed in Canada by Sterling Publishing
C/o Canadian Manda Group,
One Atlantic Avenue, Suite 105
Toronto, Ontario, Canada M6K 3E7

Every effort has been made to ensure that all the information in this book is accurate.
however, due to differing conditions, tools, and individual skills, the publisher cannot
be responsible for any injuries, losses, and other damages which may result from the
use of the information in this book.

Printed in Singapore

Sterling ISBN 0-8069-7727-2

Introduction

The creation of animal figures using origami (paper-folding) has come a long way over the past fifty years. Before that, there was a limited choice of traditional designs, with an even more limited range of available techniques. Then such American origami artists as Sam Randlett, Neil Elias, and Fred Rohm, along with the Japanese folders Akira Yoshizawa and Kunihiko Kasahara, began to develop a wide range of brand-new folding techniques. They inspired a new generation of creative folders (such as John Montroll, Robert Lang, David Brill, and Max Hulme), who have produced extraordinary works of complexity, requiring many hours of folding. Many folders acknowledge Kunihiko Kasahara to be the master of simple, elegant animal designs, and we are fortunate to be able to feature some of his work within this book.

In each chapter, projects are presented with the easiest first, and work through to more complicated models. Unless you already have some folding experience, you are recommended to practise through the designs in the order in which they appear in each chapter.

In addition to step-by-step photographs, "studio" shots show the same models made to a high standard, using alternative types of paper. These finishing touches, which create curved surfaces and a more lifelike result, are presented to inspire the folder. Origami masters are usually noted for their ability to breathe life into a fold and to imbue every model they make with a little of their own personality.

Folding Techniques

There are only two types of crease: the valley fold and the mountain fold: a valley fold (1) on one side of the paper being a mountain fold (2) on the other. Although an instruction may specify a mountain fold, you may find it easier to turn the paper over and to make a valley fold instead. It really doesn't matter as long as you return the paper to its original position so that it matches the photograph.

Similarly, the paper in the photo may have been rotated to make the fold easier.

Another tip is never to flatten a crease until you are certain it is in the right place. You will soon learn to "shuffle" the paper around so that it lines up where you want.

Although there are no formal rules about how to fold paper, there are a number of guidelines that will help you to become a better folder, as outlined below.

1. Take your time

It's easy to tell the difference between a rushed model and one that has been carefully folded. If you rush a model, it will show: creases won't be neat, edges won't line up, and corners won't be sharp. By folding slowly, you'll have more chance of learning the steps quickly.

2. Fold on a Table

Folding in the air (without sitting at a table) is difficult and has no practical advantage. It's best to fold on a table, where you can spread out the instructions and paper without feeling cramped. You can also make your creases firm by pressing them down against the table – your fingers will be enough, so you won't need any tools. Remember that folding in a quiet room is easier than in a noisy one!

3. Make Models Three Times

It's always a bit of a struggle the first time you make a model. Your brain will be trying to understand the instructions while your fingers are learning new movements. If you make the model more than once, however, it will become easier to fold every time and each finished model will look increasingly impressive. Some complex designs may need folding many times before you complete them properly.

4. Never Force the Paper into Place

If the paper isn't doing what you want, never force it into place. Instead, unfold the step you've been doing and have another look at the instructions. It also helps to check the next step to see what you're aiming for. Try to fold the paper smoothly – it may help to put your fingers inside or underneath it. Difficult moves will become easy with practice!

Seven Steps to Folding Heaven

1. Always take your time – rushed folds are rarely impressive.

2. Fold on a table in a suitable environment – not the kitchen!

3. Make all models at least three times – they'll become better with practice.

4. Never force the paper into place – unfold the step and start again instead.

5. When you learn a new model, teach it to someone.

6. Always choose attractive paper for your display models.

7. If you feel creative, follow your instincts and experiment!

5. Teach Your Model to Someone Else

Along with the joy of folding a model, there is as much fun to be had in displaying it or teaching it to someone else. A bonus is that by explaining each step you'll come to understand it much better yourself. New ways of folding may even occur to you, inspiring you to create new models. Origami's popularity has spread around the world largely because of people's willingness to teach it at any time and in any place. For many people, sharing is a central part of the origami ethic.

6. Choose Attractive Paper

Standard origami paper is perfect when it comes to practicing your models and for any initial creative work. When you are planning a model for display, however, it's worth using more impressive paper. Many types of decorative paper are sold by specialist craft stores or over the Internet, or you could use paper that isn't intended for origami – try looking in a flower shop, for example. Although you may need to cut your paper into squares, this isn't difficult, and once you've started shopping around you'll soon build up an impressive collection of paper to use for many different types of models.

7. Follow Your Instincts

You never know when the creative urge will strike: you may be on the bus, having lunch, or even lying in bed. Be prepared and always carry a supply of paper with you so that as soon as you have an idea you can explore, adapt, and repeat it. One tip is never to throw away your doodles: buy a storage box, label it "origami ideas," and store everything – however unpromising it may seem. Your unconscious mind often needs time to develop an idea, and may present you with a solution when you least expect it. Remember that you can always leave a model half-finished and come back to it later.

Creating Origami Animals

As you are folding the models in this book, you may feel inspired to make a model of a different animal. If this happens, go ahead and see what happens. After all, you can always return to the models in the book later.

There are three basic methods of creating new origami designs.

1. Some folders picture a sheet of paper in their mind and do the creating and problem-solving in their head. When they have an idea that will work, they will often fold the finished model almost immediately. This approach is not for the beginner, however, or, indeed for most creative folders.

2. Doodling involves folding a sheet of paper until something begins to emerge. This is more likely to happen if you have a wide range of folding techniques at your fingertips, which you will only learn by folding many different models and analyzing how the results have been achieved.

3. The easiest method for beginners is to simply take an existing model and change certain folds, distances, and angles. Although your model may not look very different to the original one to start with, you may eventually adapt it so much that it becomes your own creation. Do remember, however, that it is part of the origami ethic to credit the creator of the model that inspired you.

Simple Designs

A simple origami design isn't concerned with every feature of the subject animal, concentrating instead on the important parts. An elephant, for example, is essentially a gray blob with big ears and a trunk. Because the features of an origami animal are fewer than they would be in real life, their shape can be important. Where a fold has no exact location, play with the paper until it looks right to you, and only then flatten the crease. By "sketching" the subject rather than "photographing" it, you will sometimes need to use your imagination to fill in the missing details.

Simple Cat's Head

traditional variation

Start with a square of paper, white side up. By varying step 3 you can alter the proportions of the head to make other types of cat.

1. Fold in half from corner to opposite corner.

2. Fold the two narrower points up to the right-angled corner.

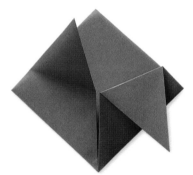

3. Fold both points back to form the ears. The side with raw edges should be approximately vertical. Both folds should start from the same place in the middle of the paper.

4. Fold the triangular corner between the ear flaps.

5. Turn over and fold over both layers of the lower right-angled corner to form the nose.

Start with a square of paper, white side up. If you hold the completed model by the ears and gently press together, the mouth will open.

1. Fold in half from corner to opposite corner and unfold.

2. Turn the paper round so the next corner faces you and fold in half from corner to corner again.

3. Turn the paper round to this position and fold the tip of the first triangle up to form the nose.

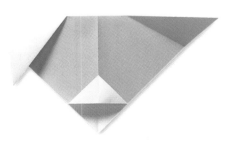

4. Fold the two sharper corners down to form ears.

5. Fold both ears back upwards, starting at the widest corners.

6. Complete!

Dollar Bill Elephant

Paul Jackson & David Mitchell

Start with a dollar bill, or similar sized paper. You can alter the first three steps to create African and Indian elephants.

1. Fold over one corner a tiny amount at a shallow angle.

2. Fold the double layer again, at the same angle.

3. Fold the nearest corner over to form the head. Don't flatten the paper until you are happy with the shape of the head. Check the next photo.

4. Fold the remaining short raw edge over and tuck it under the ear. The top corner just reaches the top of the head.

5. Fold a small triangle of paper behind at the rear end.

6. Complete!

Simple Frog's Head

Nick Robinson

Start with a square of paper, colored side up. Green paper is recommended. Hold the finished frog just in front of the eyes and gently move your hands together a little. The frog will talk!

1. Fold in half from side to opposite side, unfold and repeat with the other sides.

2. Turn the paper over to the white side and fold in half from corner to corner, crease and unfold.

3. Fold opposite (uncreased) corners to the center point.

4. Turn the paper round and fold in half so that the white squares lie on top of each other.

5. Fold one of the right-angled corners to meet the half-way point of the nearest crease.

6. Lift the triangular flap up and squash it neatly to either side. Repeat with the other corner to form the eyes.

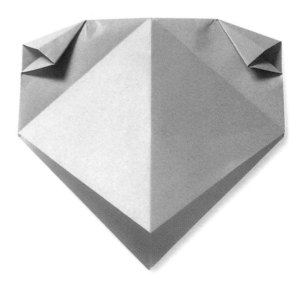

7. Complete!

Simple Dog
Nick Robinson

Start with a square of paper, white side up. Many variations are possible by altering the first two steps.

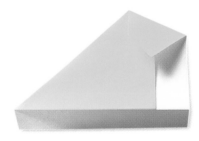

1. Fold a corner towards the opposite corner, but leave a gap of about one sixth of the distance. The exact position isn't important!

2. Fold a corner over to form the head. Adjust the angle so it matches the next photo before flattening. Once you "see" the head, this step is simple.

3. Mountain fold the white section underneath the body behind along the colored raw edge.

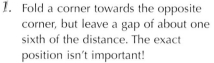

4. Turn the paper over and fold the white corner to meet the end of the colored edge.

5. Make a similar fold starting at the tip of the small triangle, to form a pointed tail.

6. Turn back over for the completed Simple Dog.

Nick Robinson

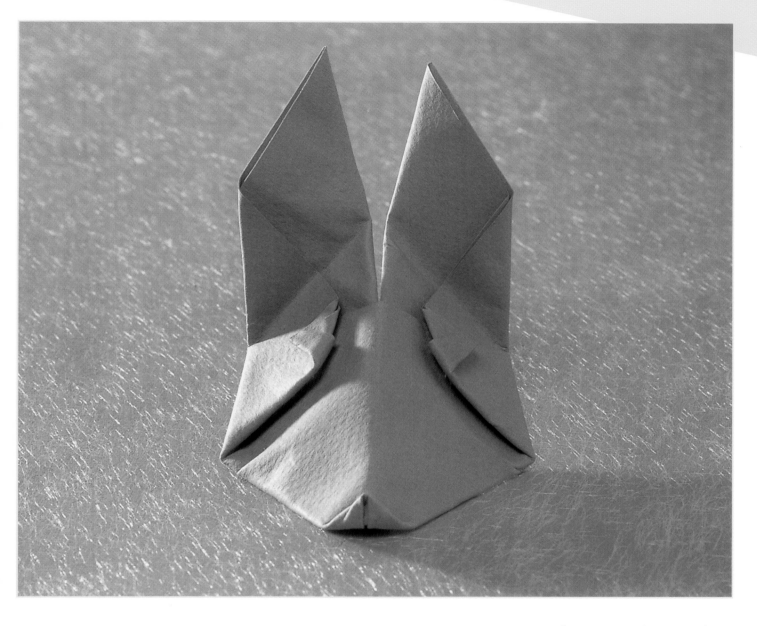

Start with a square of paper, white side up. Steps 5, 6, 7 and 9 can be varied.

1. Fold in half from corner to opposite corner, crease and unfold.

2. Turn the paper round and fold in half.

3. Turn the paper so the two loose corners are nearest. Fold both these corners to meet the half-way point of the long folded edge (marked by the crease).

4. Rotate the paper 180 degrees and fold the outer triangular flaps over the edges of the inner triangle.

5. Turn the paper over and fold the two widest corners to a point just below the center of the paper.

6. Form the eyes with small valley folds to the same two corners.

7. Fold a small corner over to form the nose. Flatten carefully, since the paper is quite thick here.

8. Turn the paper over and carefully fold the model in half down the center crease.

9. Fold both ears over at a suitable angle.

10. Complete!

Pink Pig

David Mitchell

Start with three small squares of the same size. This design is a perfect example of using simple creases to create a lifelike origami design.

1. Fold all three squares in half from corner to opposite corner.

2. Fold all three squares in half once more, crease and unfold.

3. To make the body, slide one triangle within the other until about $\frac{1}{4}$ of the inner sheet is still visible.

4. Fold the tip of the inner sheet back over the outer sheet, making sure you fold some of the outer sheet with it (this holds the body together.)

5. Leaving a small gap, fold the corners back out to form a small tail.

6. To form the head, fold the remaining triangle in half again.

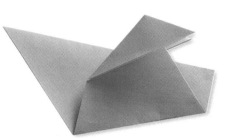

7. Checking the next photograph for guidance, fold a loose point over to meet the other folded edge at right angles. Repeat this fold behind.

8. Fold the two flaps forward to form ears.

9. The completed head.

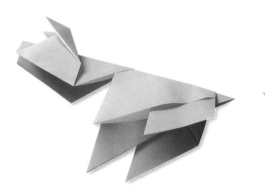

10. Slide the body between the two layers of the head.

11. Complete!

Animals

Although the folding sequence of the following designs incorporate more steps, they use the same skills as for the simple designs. I recommend that you work your way through the models, folding them in the order in which they appear in the chapter. If you can't complete any of them, don't give up – you may need to try two or three times before you are successful.

As you are working through the steps, remember to look at the next photograph to give you an idea of what you are aiming for. If the paper starts to crumple, unfold it, flatten it, and then try again. The advantage of working in a small group. folding the designs together, is that you can help each other out.

Hedgehog
Tony O'Hare

Start with a square, white side up. This design is delightfully simple, illustrating the fact that you don't need to fold every feature (in this case, the spines) to capture a subject in origami.

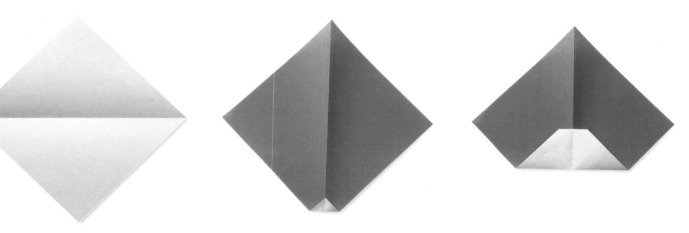

1. Fold in half from corner to opposite corner.

2. Open the fold out and turn over. Fold in a tiny flap at the end of the crease.

3. Fold the same end over again, so the inside folded edge meets the imaginary diagonal between the widest corners.

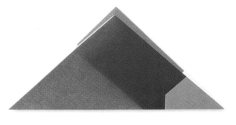

4. Turn the paper over. Starting at the half-way point of the short folded edge, fold half the edge to meet the diagonal.

5. Repeat on the other side, then fold in half on the diagonal crease made in step 1.

6. Fold the sharp corner to the right-angled corner, crease & unfold.

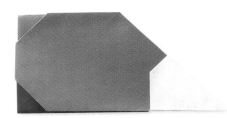

7. Fold the corner inside, tucking the inner point behind either layer of paper.

8. Fold the corner shown inside a little.

9. Repeat on the lower corner and the two matching corners underneath.

10. Fold a small part of the nose inside the model.

11. Complete!

Snake
Nick Robinson

Start with a square, white side up. For a more realistic effect, give the body of the snake some curls.

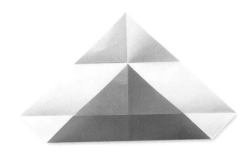

1. Fold in half from corner to corner, unfold, turn the paper round 90 degrees and repeat.

2. Fold two opposite corners to the center, crease and unfold.

3. Fold the same corners to the ³/₄ crease, crease and unfold.

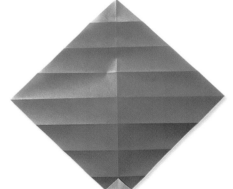

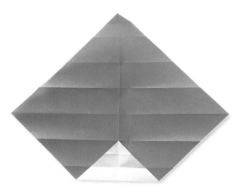

4. Fold both corners to the ¹/₄ crease, crease and unfold.

5. Turn the paper over and fold both corners to the ¹/₈ crease, crease and unfold.

6. Fold both corners to the nearest ³/₈ crease, crease and unfold.

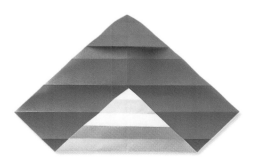

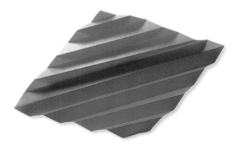

7. Fold both corners to the ⁵/₈ crease, crease and unfold.

8. Fold both corners to the ⁷/₈ crease, crease and unfold.

9. These are the final pleats, ready to form the body.

10. Use all these creases except the original diagonals to pleat the paper together.

11. Fold out two corners at one end of the strip to form eyes.

12. Mountain-fold the strip in half so the eyes are on the outside.

13. Fold the paper along the inside edge of the second white triangle, crease firmly and unfold.

14. Open the body slightly and turn the creases you've just made into valley folds. The main part of the body mountain folds in half as the head section valley folds together. This is called an "outside reverse fold".

15. Fold the head forward at a suitable angle, crease and unfold.

16. Open the layers of the head and fold both sides of the head outwards using the crease made in the last step. This is the opposite of the move in step 11 and is called an "outside reverse fold".

17. Complete!

Nick Robinson

Start with a square, white side up. The method of forming the tail can be used with many different animals.

1. Fold in half from corner to corner, crease and unfold.

2. Fold one end of the crease inwards, slightly less than $1/3$ of the length of the diagonal.

3. Fold the adjacent corners in to meet the triangle.

4. Unfold the large flap and fold the outer sides of the same flap to the center crease, crease and unfold.

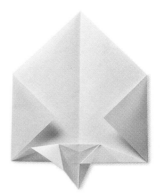

5. Swing the flap back in again and fold the inner edges of the flap in turn to the outer (folded) edge. These creases needn't pass the vertical half-way crease.

6. Fold the point of the flap back out, making the crease pass through the intersection of the creases made in the last two steps.

7. Form the tail by using the creases made in steps 4 and 5. Two new creases are formed as you flatten the paper.

8. Turn the paper over to the colored side and fold the remaining corner inwards, crease and unfold.

9. Mountain fold the model in half using an existing crease.

10. Swing the flap over, starting at the end of an existing crease, at a slight angle so the sharp corner lies above the back. Check the photo carefully! Crease and unfold.

11. The crease you have just made needs to become a valley crease and the crease made in step 8 a mountain crease. Use these two creases to fold the head in between the layers of the body.

12. Fold the tip of the head outwards to form a nose (already shown in step 11), flattening the body when complete.

13. Complete!

Start with a square, white side up. The neck may take a little practise, but is a very useful fold and worth the effort.

1. Fold in half from corner to corner, crease and unfold.

2. Fold two adjacent sides in to the center crease.

3. Turn the paper over and fold over the triangular part of the kite shape.

4. Open the flaps folded in step two.

5. Fold them to meet the triangular flap.

6. Unfold all flaps and turn the paper over.

7. Reform the kite shape with the two flaps folded down.

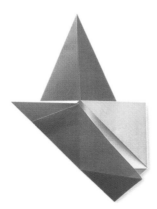

8. Fold the white triangular flap in half, extending the crease to the edge of the paper. Repeat with the matching flap.

9. Use only existing creases to form a triangular flap in the center. Check next photo for guidance.

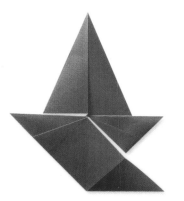

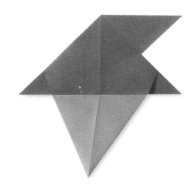

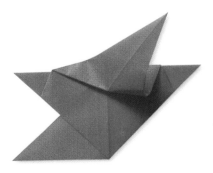

10. Flatten this flap to one side and turn the paper over.

11. Fold the narrow flap backwards along an edge underneath.

12. Make a short crease to the center at the base of the triangular flap.

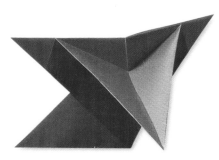

13. Repeat the crease on the other side and put both creases in at the same time as you mountain fold the body in half.

14. Fold the tip over to form a head, crease and unfold.

15. Fold the head section inside using existing creases. This is an inside-reverse fold (see Snake.)

16. Fold the tip of the head underneath before flattening the head again.

17. Fold the back corner over to form a tail.

18. Complete!

Bat

Nick Robinson

Start with a square, white side up. You can create a very realistic bat by curving the edges between the wing angles.

1. Fold in half from corner to opposite corner.

2. Fold in half again, crease and unfold.

3. Fold the long folded edge to just below the top of the triangle.

4. Fold the same triangle over the folded edge, leaving a slight gap.

5. Mountain fold the model in half behind.

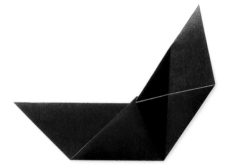

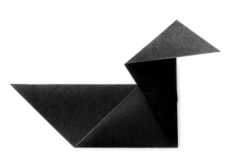

6. Make a crease which starts at the bottom corner and meets the angle formed at the back of the head.

7. Fold the two lower sides of the wing together.

8. Fold the tip of the wing down on a crease which joins the two wider corners.

9. Repeat the last three steps on the other wing.

10. Open the wings, but don't flatten the paper.

11. Complete!

Panda

Sy Chen

Start with a square of black/white paper. This design is a good exercise in careful creasing and folding.

1. Fold from corner to opposite corner, crease and unfold.

2. Repeat with the remaining two corners.

3. Fold one corner in ¹/₃ of the distance from corner to corner. You can either measure this, or fold it so that the black section is the same width as the remaining white section.

4. Fold the other corner to overlap the first. Adjust the last step if really necessary!

5. Turn the paper over and make a pinch-mark between the two angled corners.

6. Make a similar fold, taking the corner to the most recent crease and pinching lightly.

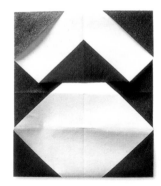

7. Now fold the most recent pinch mark so that it lies along the original half-way crease.

8. Fold the remaining corner to the crease made in step 5

9. Fold the loose corner upwards as shown.

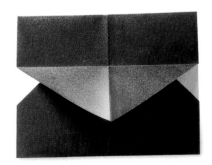

10. Then back down again, leaving a gap.

11. Form the nose with another small crease.

12. Turn the paper over and carefully fold the two corners as far out as they will go.

13. This is the result.

14. Fold the triangular flaps inwards.

15. Then back out, leaving a small gap, to form ears. Turn the paper over.

16. Complete!

Start with a square of green/white paper, white side up. Tony is a Welshman who has a special interest in frogs.

1. Fold in half from side to side, crease and unfold. Repeat on both sides.

2. Turn the paper over and fold from corner to opposite corner both ways. Fold the left and right center creases towards you, flattening the paper into a triangle.

3. This is the result, known as a "waterbomb" base.

4. Fold one point to the top of the triangle.

5. Fold the double layered outside edge to the inside edge, crease firmly & unfold back to step 3.

6. Use only existing creases and start to collapse the paper as shown. One small crease becomes a mountain crease.

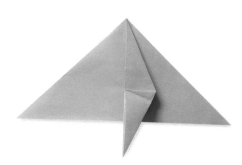

7. This is the result. Swing the narrow flap towards you.

8. Now fold the flap back along its outside edge - check the next photo carefully.

9. Repeat steps 4 to 8 on the other flap to produce this result. Fold the right-hand point and adjoining flap to the left

10. Then swing the lower triangular flap from left to right underneath.

11. Fold the triangular flap over.

12. Then fold it back to start the back leg - check the next photo.

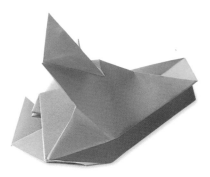

13. Complete the back leg with another angled crease. Repeat steps 12 and 13 for the other leg.

14. Fold all layers of the square corner over, crease firmly and unfold.

15. Push one corner within the model to form a small pocket, then tuck the matching triangle into the pocket and flatten the body.

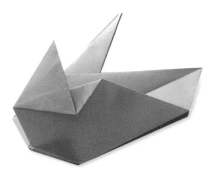

16. This is the result – the last two steps "lock" the back of the model together.

17. Complete!

Frog with Tadpoles

Tadpole
Nick Robinson

Start with a square of black/white paper. Narrowing and shaping the tail in steps 5 & 6 will take a little practise to perfect.

1. Fold from corner to opposite corner, crease and unfold.

2. Fold a side to lie along the diagonal, but move the tip of the corner you are folding *away* from the open corner a little, so that the other end of the crease doesn't quite touch the corner. Check the photo carefully before flattening. Repeat on the other side.

3. Fold the narrow point to the opposite corner.

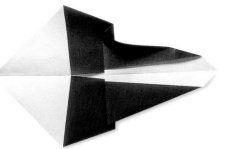

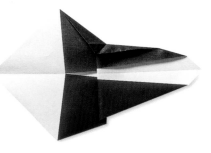

4. Leave a small gap and fold the point back again.

5. Start to narrow the sides of the tail towards the center as shown, the paper won't flatten at this stage.

6. At the same time, fold in and flatten the paper on the layer underneath. Put your fingers into the flaps to help the fold flatten smoothly.

7. Repeat on the other side and fold the model in half. It's easier from here onwards!

8. Fold the sharp corner to the right-angled corner.

9. Fold the triangular flap in half, crease and unfold the last two steps.

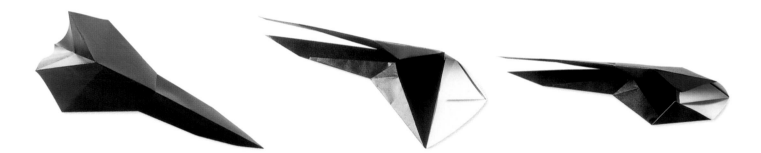

10. Fold the paper inside using existing creases. This is an inside reverse fold (see the head of the Horse, p31.)

11. Fold over the flap inside using the crease made in step 9.

12. Shape the body by folding small flaps inside. Round the body & add a curl to the tail.

13. Complete!

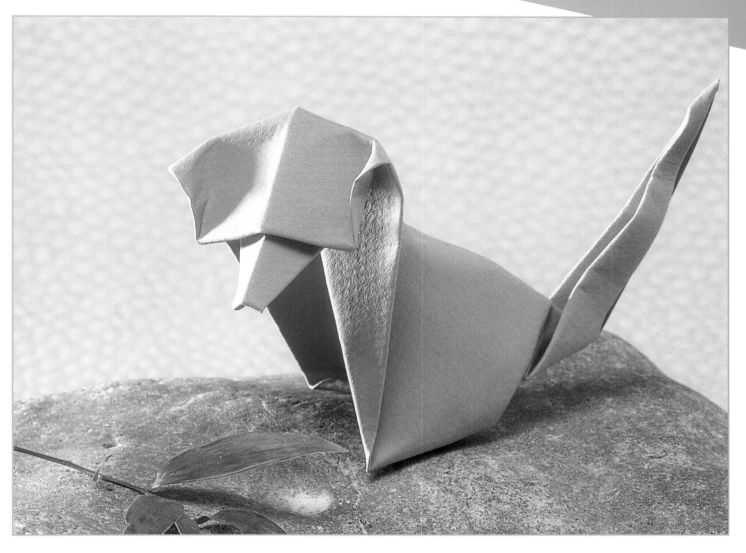

Start with a square, white side up. Kasahara is a master of origami: his designs are a delight to fold and look at.

1. Crease a diagonal, then fold two adjacent sides in to the center crease.

2. Fold the two remaining raw edges to the center as well.

3. Fold a point over, making the crease pass through the point where the flaps meet at the center.

4. Fold the flap back out, lining the crease up with the two widest points. Then fold the short, inner edges to meet the vertical edge, crease and unfold.

5. Narrow the tail to the center on both sides, flattening the paper at the top using creases made in the last step (see the tail of the Bloodhound, p29.)

6. Fold the model in half and start to fold the sharp flap to the right, starting at the lower-left corner.

7. Open the pocket and start to carefully flatten the point.

8. This is the result.

9. Form the base by folding two flaps within the model.

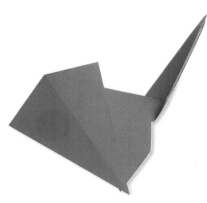

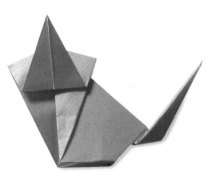

10. Open the tail and fold it outwards and upwards, making an outside reverse fold (see Snake, p26.)

11. Fold the sharp point upwards on the head.

12. Blunt the tip with a small valley fold.

13. Make a mountain fold to swing the "nose" flap inside, leaving a small gap.

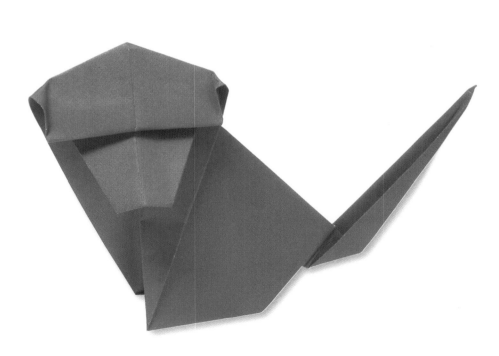

14. Open the ears with gentle creases and round the nose.

15. Complete!

Rhino

Nick Robinson

Start with three squares of the same color and size, white side up. Crease both diagonals on all three sheets. This looks like a complex design, but it isn't really - just read the instructions carefully throughout. The design can be made into 3D with a few careful creases at the end.

Body (both sections)

1. Fold in half on a diagonal.

2. Fold the long (folded) edge over about one third of the way.

3. Fold the small triangular flaps inwards.

4. Fold the inside edges of the small triangular flaps over to lie on the outside edge. Repeat on the other flap, crease firmly and unfold.

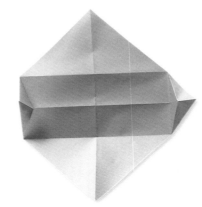

5. Reform the small creases as shown to form the feet.

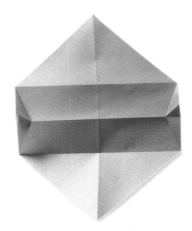

6. This is the result - fold another sheet to this stage.

Body (tail)

1. Mountain fold the paper in half behind

2. Fold the upper flap over so that the raw edges meet the inside corners of the feet.

3. Fold the lower flap over on an existing crease, then fold a flap back to form the tail.

Body (front)

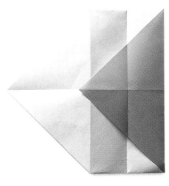

1. Turn the paper over to the white side.

2. Fold a corner inwards. Fold the center section in half again, creasing through the top layer, then unfold.

3. Fold the tip of the colored flap inside using the crease you have just made, fold over the tip inside again if necessary.

Body (assembly)

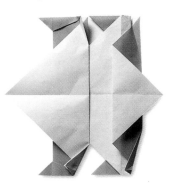

1. Place the tail section on top of the front section, tucking the white triangle behind to "lock" the body together.

2. Pleat the large white section over the layered section.

3. Narrow the back of the legs (make these creases firm!)

4. Fold the white triangular flap over to lie along an edge underneath.

5. Finally, fold the body in half. You might like to try shaping the body to make it more three-dimensional.

Head

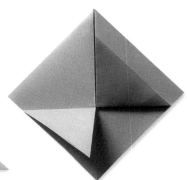

1. Fold the square in half on a diagonal, then fold two sharper corners to meet the (right-angled) third corner.

2. Fold the two points back about ³/₄ of the way

3. Fold the remaining corner back about ¹/₃ of the way.

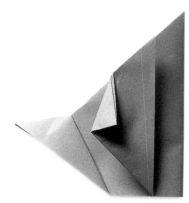

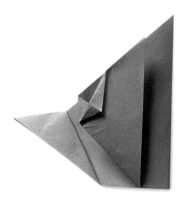

4. Make two angled crease to form the horn (see neck of the Horse, p31) then mountain fold the head in half.

5. Fold two flaps over just behind the horn.

6. Form eyes by opening and squashing the tip of the eye flap (see the eyes on the Frog's Head, p14.)

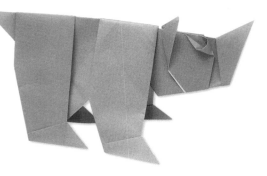

7. Narrow the head by folding two flaps underneath.

8. Fold the ears over on either side. Tuck the head within the pocket of the body to complete the model.

Giraffe
Nick Robinson

Start with a square, white side up. This design has some folds which may be easier to do "in the air" rather than flat on the table. Open the front legs a little to help it stand upright.

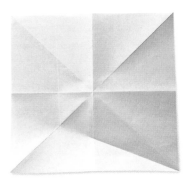

1. Fold from corner to opposite corner both ways, crease and unfold.

2. Fold in half from side to side both ways, crease and unfold.

3. Turn the paper over and fold a side to the nearest diagonal crease, but only crease as far as the half way crease.

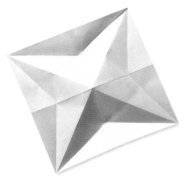

4. This is the result after you have repeated the last fold seven more times! Refold in half from the colored side.

5. Use the existing creases to swing the paper towards you.

6. Carefully flatten the paper. This should feel natural, if not, unfold and check your creases.

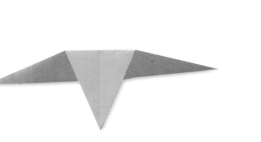

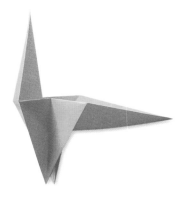

7. Repeat the fold behind.

8. Open the paper slightly and carefully swing one of the long flaps upwards.

9. Narrow the point at a slight angle, repeating behind.

10. Fold the neck flap over on both sides.

11. Fold the back leg flap over so the tip lines up with the base of the front legs. Crease and unfold.

12. Open the flap out and make an outside reverse fold. (see the head of the Snake, p26.)

13. Fold the head over at a suitable angle, crease firmly and unfold.

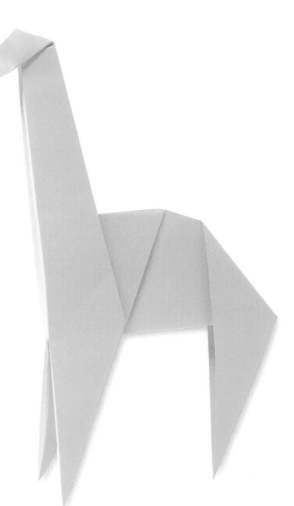

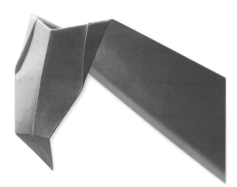

14. Make an outside reverse fold to form the head, then fold the tip of the nose underneath.

15. Complete!

Start with a square, white side up. This model is a little more difficult, but not impossible! You may need to make it several times to master the folding techniques. For first attempts, you can use a slightly larger square.

1. Start with a diagonal, then fold two adjacent sides in to the center crease.

2. Fold the short edges to the center, crease and unfold.

3. Reverse fold the same flaps inside - look closely at the photograph.

4. Mountain fold the model in half.

5. Fold the smaller triangular flap to about the half-way point of the opposite edge.

6. Fold the same flap back at an angle which starts at the top corner. This will determine the shape of the head.

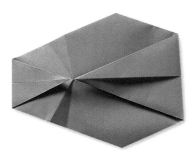

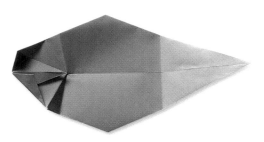

7. Unfold and open the body from underneath. Fold both corners to the crease mark shown. Unfold the longer corner.

8. Narrow the head section as shown - if the paper is quite thick, leave a small gap at the tip of the nose.

9. Swivel the head section backwards on existing creases. (this is the opposite of the head folds in the Bloodhound, p.29.)

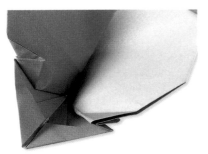

10. Look inside the head and "lock" the head section in place with valley folds.

11. Fold the ear flap backwards at an angle.

12. Tuck the ear behind the head flap. Repeat the last two steps with the other ear. Carefully fold the tip of the nose over.

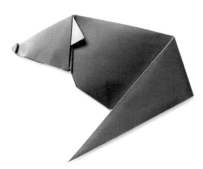

13. Fold the tail, starting at the top of an existing crease, so the top of the tail touches the lower front corner. Crease firmly and unfold.

14. Open the tail and fold it inside the body using existing creases.

15. Carefully narrow both sides of the tail.

16. Complete!

Cotton-tailed rabbit

Nick Robinson

Start with a square, white side upwards. Once again, fold slowly and carefully. For first attempts, use a slightly larger square.

1. Fold from side to side, crease and unfold, both ways.

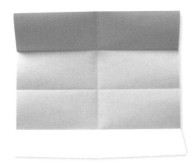

2. Fold two opposite sides to the center, crease and unfold.

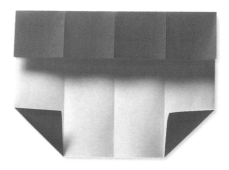

3. Fold a third side in to the center, crease and unfold. Then fold two corners in to meet the quarter creases.

4. Swing the two sides to the centre on existing creases.

5. Fold the upper short edge to the center on an existing crease.

6. Fold the loose corners of the shorter flap to the middle of the top edge, crease and unfold. Swing the flap upwards again.

7. Fold the inner corners of the upper layer back to the center. A triangular flap is formed.

8. Fold the tip of the nose over. Take a deep breath, you're doing fine!

9. Swing the ear flaps over the nose.

10. Turn the paper over and fold it in half.

11. Fold the sharp corner over so that the edge lies along the original half-way crease. Crease firmly and unfold.

12. Open out the body.

13. Fold the "nose" flap over, then turn the paper over.

14. Make the two "angled" creases into valley creases (one is already). Then fold two short edges to meet the valley creases.

15. Fold the body in half underneath, at the same time fold the head section backwards using the valley creases mentioned in the last step. Allow the nose flap to swing forwards. Fold this step slowly, checking the next photograph for guidance.

16. The head is now complete. Fold the white corner to meet the lower edge of the original half-way crease.

17. Fold the white flap back on itself, starting the crease at the corner shown.

18. Open the tail section out and fold the corners in to meet the nearest crease.

19. Swing the tail flap upwards as you start to flatten the body.

20. Carefully narrow the tail section.

21. Round the lower corner by folding a flap behind on either side. Open and round the tail.

Dinosaurs

Here are a selection of prehistoric designs for you to make. Some of them are ideal for experimenting with - try to adapt them to create your own designs. Once you know how to fold them, try to find impressive paper to fold with and see if you can arrange them into a "Jurassic" scene. You could even use a digital camera and present it on a website!

Simple Mammoth

Nick Robinson

Start with a square, white side upwards. This design is a variation of the Simple Dog.

1. Fold a corner over towards the opposite corner, leaving a small gap.

2. Fold one corner over to form the head - check the next photograph as a guide and don't flatten until you're happy.

3. Fold a section of the tail behind.

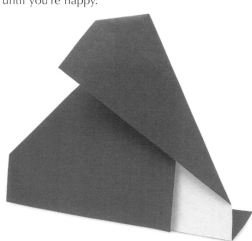

4. Fold the white section at the base behind to form a stand.

5. Complete!

Start with a square, colored side down. All angles and distances can be varied.

Version 1

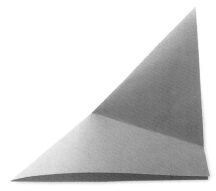

1. Fold in half from corner to opposite corner.

2. Fold part of the paper up and to the right (check the next photo.) The two edge overlap at right angles, more or less!

3. Fold the raw corner flaps up to match the next photo.

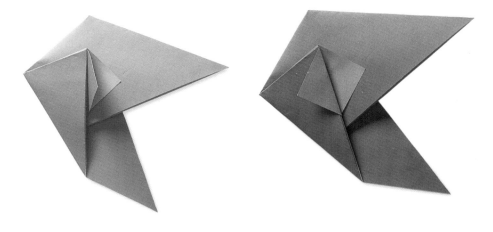

4. Fold the top flap over to form an eye.

5. Complete!

Version 2

1. Fold in half from corner to opposite corner.

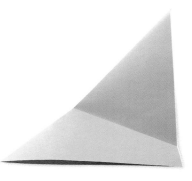

2. Fold part of the paper up and to the right, the same as with the last model.

3. This is the result.

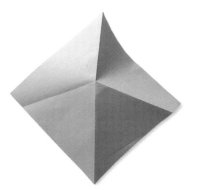

4. Open the paper a little - you need to change the shorter valley crease into a mountain crease.

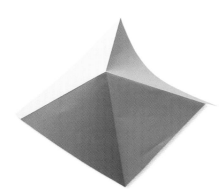

5. Then make the long mountain crease into a valley crease. This forms an inside reverse fold. (See the head of the Tadpole, p44.)

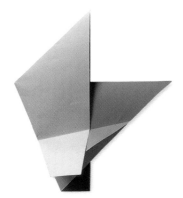

6. Fold up the flap with the raw corner to form an eye. Turn the paper over and repeat this move on the other side.

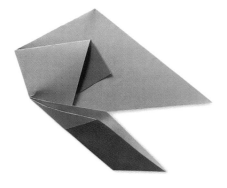

7. Fold the jaw over at a suitable angle, crease and unfold.

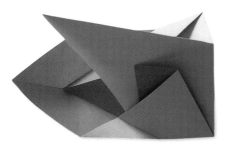

8. Open the lower jaw and make an outside reverse fold using existing creases.

9. Complete!

Start with a square, white side up. Hold the flaps at the back of the head and move them apart to open & close the beak.

1. Fold in half from corner to corner & unfold.

2. Fold two sides in to meet the diagonal.

3. Fold the short raw edges in to the center, crease firmly and unfold.

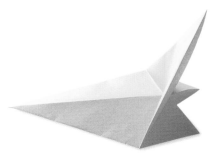

4. Inside reverse along these creases (identical to step 3 of the Mouse, p59.)

5. Fold the small triangular flaps over on a hidden layer, then tuck them within the pocket underneath.

6. Make a valley crease along the shorter section of the paper, at the same time make a mountain fold along the center of the longer section. This forms an outside reverse fold (see the head of the Giraffe, p56.)

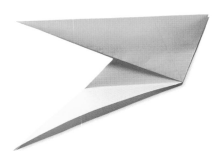

7. Fold the point of the inside flap to meet the point of the outside flap. Crease firmly.

8. Undo the last fold, the make an outside reverse fold on existing creases. (See Baby dinosaur head, p68.)

9. Complete!

Nick Robinson

Start with a 2 by 1 rectangle (half a square), white side up. The same design could be made by folding a square in half, but half the paper would be wasted.

1. Fold the two short edges together.

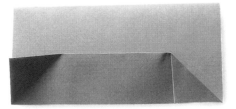

2. Rotate the paper, then fold both raw edges back to the folded edge, one on either side.

3. Fold the raw edges in half again, on either side.

4. Fold the inside corners over to meet the raw edge.

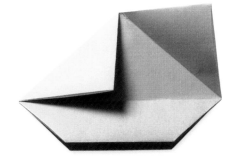

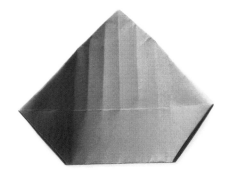

5. Then unfold the corners and inside reverse fold them (see step 4 of the Pteradon head, p69.) Repeat behind.

6. Swing the leg section down on either side, then fold the raw edges to meet the horizontal crease.

7. Turn the paper over and add some vertical creases (to look like fins).

8. Fold the leg sections back up on either side and swing one leg flap to face the other way. Repeat behind.

9. Fold all four legs down at similar angles.

10. Complete!

Dinosaur Group

T-Rex

Nick Robinson

Start with a square, white side up, with a diagonal crease. This design and the Apatosaurus share many folds, yet have totally different results.

1. Fold two adjacent sides in to meet the diagonal.

2. Fold the short raw edges in to the center, crease firmly and unfold.

3. Inside reverse fold these two flaps, as with the Pteradon head, p69.

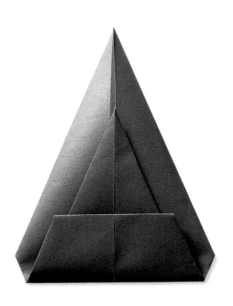

4. Fold the triangular flap over the raw edges.

5. Leaving a small gap, fold the flap back again.

6. Fold the paper over as shown.

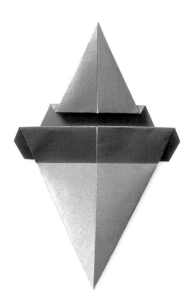

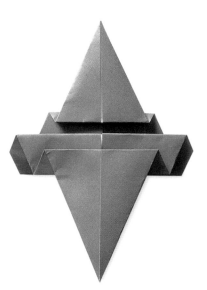

7. Turn the paper over and fold the flap back as shown.

8. Turn the paper over once more and fold the larger (tail) flap inside along the edge underneath.

9. Then fold it back out again, leaving a small gap.

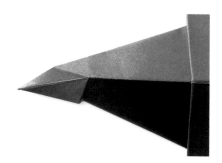

10. Mountain fold the model in half, then open the layers of the head and flatten to one side.

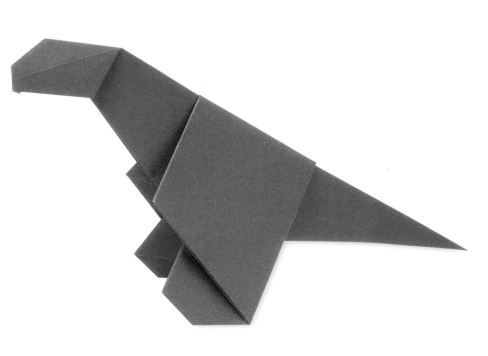

11. Fold the tip of the nose inside.

12. Complete!

Nick Robinson

Start with a square, white side up, with a diagonal crease. Like the T-Rex, this design can be made more realistic by carefully flattening the back to make it three dimensional.

1. Fold two adjacent sides in to meet the diagonal.

2. Fold the short raw edges in to the center, crease firmly and unfold.

3. Inside reverse fold these two flaps, as with the T-Rex.

4. Fold the inside corners out as shown (these are the back legs), then fold the model in half.

5. Fold the sharp flap just over the end of the back legs.

6. Fold the same flap back at a slight angle.

7. Fold the other long point back at an angle.

8. Turn the paper round, then fold the same point forwards again, starting at the base of the front leg.

9. Use the creases made to fold both head and tail in and out again (see the head of the Bloodhound, p29).

10. Open the layers at the end of the neck and flatten to one side, forming the head.

11. Fold the tip of the nose inside.

12. Complete!

Credits and Acknowledgements

Thanks to Sarah and David King and David Petty for realizing this book; to David Mitchell, Kunihiko Kasahara, Sy Chen, Tony O'Hare, and Paul Jackson for allowing their designs to be published; to Alison, Daisy, Nick, Gomez, and Matilda for being my beautiful family; and to paper-folders everywhere for their love and inspiration.

Origami Contacts

If you've enjoyed folding the projects in this book, contact your nearest origami society, which will supply you with paper, new designs, a newsletter, and, most importantly, many new friends!

Origami Websites

Origami U.S.A.: www.origami-usa.org
British Origami Society: www.britishorigami.org.uk
The author's website is www.12testing.net